Small Conflicts

Mareska Chettiar

BookLeaf Publishing

India | USA | UK

Presentation by *BookLeaf Publishing*

Web: www.bookleafpub.com

E-mail: info@bookleafpub.com

ISBN: 9789358314946

First edition 2023

DEDICATION

To Mumma, for loving and supporting me every damn day.

ACKNOWLEDGEMENT

Big thanks to Vernon Muthu for making the cover, and Faith Zantua for proofreading and editing!

PREFACE

And if the world ended and there was only one person alive, I pray they weren't a poet.

7:42am After A Sleepless Night

There is a stabbing conflict within me.
One that is spurred by loneliness—
A loneliness of the heart.
But what could ever sate it?

The conflict goes something like this:
I wake alone in my bed, cold and wanting.
Yet I am too young, too naïve.

I long for someone who'll
Complete me, fill me, save me,
Not realizing they're an accessory—
Not necessity.

And so the conflict continues,
Running circles around my heart
As I cry myself to sleep,
Cold, wanting, young, naïve,
Lonely.

Lonely enough to write this
As a prayer to my future self,
To endure this conflict
And hope there's a reward waiting

At another beginning.

I Was Left Alone for Too Long

How am I different than the billions that came
before me?
I stand alone, solitary in a universe,
Cruel in its impossibility.
How can I be a cumulation of everything
And subsequently mean nothing?
What impact could a measly existence have
On the infinity of the universe?
It would be absurd to call me a speck.
But somehow, I am alive.
Where do I even start making meaning of it?
What I am to say to a world
Created from nothing,
In which I reside, barely breathing,
Trying to comprehend that my life is miserable,
Insignificant,
But overwhelmingly my everything?
How do I go on knowing that every tiny thing I
do,
Every minute of the day,
Changes absolutely nothing? Means nothing?
In a few years I will be gone,
My writings forgotten, my legacy dissipating.
So what was the point?

And if there was no point,
Why do my feelings encompass me so?

Escape

There's this daydream I have.
I think about it often.
More often than I should,
Since daydreams are desperate wishes,
A short escape from a miserable life.

So I retreat into it every chance I get—
Into a warm, golden evening
With a gentle breeze
And delicious, baked scents.
I think I'm on a picnic.

The sunset is almost blinding,
And I am oddly comfortable—
Suspiciously happy.
I realize I am not alone;
The source of my contentedness
Is someone beside me.

And I stare at them for a bit,
Into their welcoming, curious eyes.
A small tilt graces the corner of their lips
As if they find me adorable,
Even amusing.
I am obsessed.

This dream doesn't end—
I revisit it often,
Building where I left off.
Sometimes we are married.
Sometimes I tell them my deepest fear.

And then I am dragged back into reality
Where sunsets aren't romantic
And there's no time for picnics.
But somehow, their face persists
Silently encouraging,
And reality doesn't seem as daunting.

Companionship

I want someone who's going to sit
And listen to me read poetry for hours.
Poetry that I poured my heart and soul into.
Poetry that reflects every piece of me.
I want to see every emotion that graces their
features,
I want to hear every thought they form from my
words.
I want them to be absorbed in my sorrow—
So much that their tears reflect
The old, dried ones soaked in paper.
I want them to smile.
I want them to come over,
And hug me because they couldn't be there
At my lowest.
They'd hug me because they were glad
I was breathing, thriving—
Glad that I pushed past evil.

And I'd hug them back.
Because I knew, without doubt,
That they loved me with every droplet of their
existence
And that they'd fight time to ease my pain.

I'd hug them because they heard me
And did not run.

I've Moved On, I Really Have

I'm cold.
All of a sudden,
I thought about him.
It sent shivers up my spine,
And irritated me to no end.
I don't want to go through this again.
Though his presence engulfed by being,
My every thought and prayer—
I refuse to let it continue any longer.
I refuse to give him dominion
Over a life he hasn't spared a thought to.

I have a weird feeling in my chest.
So strong that I barely stopped
From checking in on him,
From destroying my facade of nonchalance.
But it was enough to make me think
And wonder if he remembers me
And our nights together

Maybe, if the universe was a little more cruel
I could be with him
And he could watch my love that still bleeds—
A stream that runs infinitely, unappreciated.

Calculated

I liked to live life calculated.
Predicting outcomes and steps;
Making the most logical decisions.

And then I fell in love.

The thing with love is,
You throw yourself into the pit
And feel every spike as you are impaled,
Over and over and over,
And wonder if it was worth it.

Love is chaos at its finest.

Wrong

My eyes are tired,
But my mind will not rest.
I'm thinking of all the "wrongs".
People I have wronged,
Words I cannot take back,
Places I shouldn't have been.
Regret splashes every corner of my heart.
All things that ended badly,
All things that made me hurt.
What would I change
If I had the chance?
If I could make my "what if's" a reality?

Instead, I roll over,
And shake my head feebly.
The past cannot change,
But I could wake up,
Just a tiny bit more refreshed
Tomorrow, with the sun smiling—
I could step forward.

Conformity

I hate it when people laugh at me.
It haunts me longer than it probably should.

Ridicule.

What could someone possibly do to deserve it?

Perhaps, just existing is reason enough.

Brother? I'm Sorry.

The word "brother"
Means the world to me.
Maybe because I never had any—
Or maybe because I had too many.
It carries a world of hurt,
A world of laughter,
And a barren world—
The one where we are far, far apart.

Brother, do you still remember me?

How am I supposed to tell you
I miss you more than I dare say?
How can I reach out
When time keeps running
Forward, faster, stronger,
Ramming into me,
Leaving me hurt and breathless,
Leaving carnage in its wake.

What will it be like
When I meet your eyes again?
Will I feel guilt, shame,
Or an overwhelming sense of relief?

Brother,
Do you still remember me?

I'm Not Sure if I Wish I Forgot, or if I'm Happy I Remember

There are times in my childhood
I refuse to think about.
Times where malice ran rampant.
Times where good was rendered powerless.
But no matter how hard I try—
The memories remain crystal clear,
And the pain feels so real.
It's like I'm seven again.
Pulled by the hair into the living room,
Tears streaming down my face,
Too terrified to even beg.
My sister is beside me,
We were having a kid's spat.
But we were too loud,
Too much like children,
And that spat led to us
Down on cold, hard floor,
Shaking—
As rage and terror swept the room.
We slept there that night.
I don't remember what happened after.
It probably went the way it always did:

We sucked it up and moved on,
While the culprit remained void
Of responsibility,
Maybe even remorse.
It's saddening how even time
Fails to change the monstrosities
Oblivious to what they are.

Fortress, Me

It's a little about choices,
A little about life.
It's a little about conditioning,
A little about strife.
Personality and pain.
Growth in the pouring rain—
An intense buildup of disdain.
Where does it all go?

How can I, a crumbling fortress,
Hold the weight of the world on my weathered
bricks?
I want to end my run,
But have so much longer to go—
Past wounds keep me afloat,
Amidst my crumbling walls.
The foundation holds surprisingly strong,
Comfortably solid on shaky ground.

Morals slowly build the walls anew,
With past and present scattered askew.
Renewed but forever old,
Foundation strong, gated, and bold.

Emotionally

The beauty of nature,
The gift of life.
Was it a simple happening,
Or an intended creation?

Maybe one day,
A couple thousand years ago,
A tiny tug,
A little string that showed
Not only relation, but recognition
Slowly surfaced.
And hence, feelings were born.
And from those feelings,
Came love.
But did us creatures create love?
Perhaps to find another reason to survive.
Or maybe it was an accident—
A sudden realization.
Did we make love?
Or was it given to us?

Perhaps a higher being did it
Just to toy with us,
Bestowing us with an emotion so strong,
Nations fell at its feet.

Though I'm just a tiny speck singing,
And these songs will fade, very soon,
That tug will remain—
And hence, your tears will not go unheard,
Your grievances not ignored.

Burden

When you're badly hurt,
You sort of carry it around with you.
Sometimes, it bleeds all over everything else.
And at other times, you feel the hurt chipping
away,
Gradually getting lighter.
It takes months, even years,
For it to slowly erode,
Leaving nothing but a vague memory.

But there's always new hurts and wounds
And new burdens and bleeds.
Tell me, what do I do if
I'm taking on weight faster and faster
Than I could ever let it fade?

Weathered

Blood drips through my soul.
It is hollow.
I messed up, and now everything is scrambled.
I wonder if it even has meaning anymore.

And yet I will wake up and move as if nothing
happened.

As if every day isn't me fighting to find purpose,
Hoping that if i move enough, maybe,
Just maybe,
Everything will fix itself,
Fall into place.
I won't have to walk through fog
Where unsuspecting traps ensnare me—

I am tired.

Done with having to pretend like nothing
happened,
Like it didn't affect me,
Like it didn't take a piece of my soul
To smile immediately after,
Knowing that no consequences will appear
Eternally.

Infinite Loop

What would a perfect mind be like?
Would it toil over life like I do?

Would I waste no time,
Be rich,
Successful,
Beautiful,
And everything that society wants?

Or would I be the opposite—
Secluded,
Silent,
Scarce,
Breaking free?

What would a perfect mind pick?
Why?

Trailing Blood

I feel like I'm not doing enough.
Like I have to take up everything,
Be good at it,
Not complain,
Not falter,
And smile.

I'm lagging behind while everyone is miles
ahead,
Laughing at my pace.
Laughing, together.
I continue my lonely hobble.

Pieces

I've met some split people in my life.
Sometimes they say,
"Hey, how are you today?"
And sometimes it's like,
"Get the hell out of my way!"
I wonder why they're that way.
The splinter I come to meet
Really just depends on the day.

Sometimes I feel like they're hiding.
Though I wonder if the reasons I seek
Are worth finding.
They seem to think their splitness
Is worth priding.
Maybe ignoring the hurt they spread
Is how they make up for their crying.

I wonder what finally split them.

Dip Below. Please.

Why? Why? Why?
Everyone's focusing on the what
And never the why.
Everyone's focusing on the happening
And never the cause.
Maybe if we were to think
A little— just a little—
About the origins and the wrongs,
We'd have to partake in an exhausting cycle,
One where you'd have to leave
A room of comfort for a room of conflict.
One where you'd have to face the darkest
corners
Of not only the world, but yourself.
So we sit and do nothing,
Happy on the surface.
But really, why?

From the River to the Sea

Dark souls roam the earth.
I never understood dread
Until I met one.
They stand with evil.
They find justification in the unspeakable—
Always looking for a technicality,
A minor complication.
Always ignoring the larger horror.

Somehow,
Reason is rendered pointless.
Lives turned numbers, ridiculed.
The privileged stay silent.
The advocates are ostracized.
Dark souls run rampant.
The white doves are burning.
Power looks away.

Depart

You came,
You made art,
And you left.

And that was enough.